Securing Tomorrow's World: Exploring the Convergence of Cybersecurity, Quantum Computing and AI

Aeron P. White

Copyright © 2024 Aeron P. White

All rights reserved.

ISBN-13: 979-8-3243-8648-1

For my wife, Rita, who was often the light in my darkness.

CONTENTS

	Acknowledgments	i
	Foreword from the Author	1
1	The Origins of Cybersecurity: A Brief History	4
2	Today's Computers	10
3	Securing the Present: Cybersecurity with Today's Computers	20
4	Quantum Computing: New Beginnings	24
5	Quantum Cryptography Overview	30
6	Securing the Future: Quantum Computing Cybersecurity	35
7	Understanding Quantum Threats	40
8	Unleashing the Potential: The Future of AI with Quantum Computers	44
9	Exploring the Future Frontiers of Computing	49
10	Exploring the Potential Threat to Humanity's Survival	80
11	Epilogue: Charting the Path Forward	86

ACKNOWLEDGMENTS

Thanks go to ChatGPT3.5 for valuable research material.

FOREWORD FROM THE AUTHOR

In the ever-evolving landscape of technology, few topics hold as much intrigue and promise as the convergence of cybersecurity, quantum computing, and artificial intelligence. As we stand at the precipice of a new era defined by unprecedented connectivity and computational power, the need to understand and navigate the complexities of these intersecting domains has never been more pressing.

In "Securing Tomorrow's World: Exploring the Convergence of Cybersecurity, Quantum Computing and AI" we embark on a captivating journey into the heart of this convergence, offering a comprehensive exploration of the synergies, challenges, and implications that lie at the nexus of cybersecurity, quantum computing and AI. With attention to detail and a view to emerging trends, we attempt to illuminate the cutting-edge technologies, groundbreaking research and transformative applications that are reshaping our world.

From the intricacies of quantum cryptography to the ethical considerations of AI-driven cybersecurity, this book traverses a diverse landscape of topics, inviting readers to delve into the depths of innovation and discovery. Through insightful analysis and thought-provoking prose, we attempt to provide invaluable insights into the opportunities and risks inherent in this rapidly evolving field.

But this book is more than a mere exploration of technological advancements—it is a call to action. As we harness the power of quantum computing and AI to tackle some of society's most pressing challenges, we must also confront the ethical, legal, and societal implications of our innovations. With great power comes great responsibility, and it is incumbent upon us to ensure that the benefits of these technologies are equitably distributed and ethically deployed.

As we embark on a journey through the pages of this book, you are encouraged to approach each chapter with an open mind and a spirit of inquiry. For in the convergence of cybersecurity, quantum computing, and AI lies the promise of a brighter, more secure future for generations to come. May "Securing Tomorrow's World: Exploring the Convergence of Cybersecurity, Quantum Computing and AI" serve as both a guide and an inspiration as we navigate the complexities of our digital age, but it also comes with a twist, an irony, since the Author was aptly supported by state-of-the-art AI in sourcing the content for this book.

1 THE ORIGINS OF CYBERSECURITY: A BRIEF HISTORY

Cybersecurity, the practice of protecting computer systems, networks, and data from unauthorized access, manipulation, and destruction, has its roots in the early days of computing. The evolution of cybersecurity can be traced back to several key milestones and developments throughout history.

Image: AI impression of the origins of Cybersecurity

Securing Tomorrow's World: Exploring the Convergence of Cybersecurity, Quantum Computing and AI

1.1 The Birth of Computing

The origins of cybersecurity can be linked to the advent of modern computing in the mid-20th century. With the invention of the first electronic computers, such as the ENIAC and UNIVAC, came the need to secure these machines from physical tampering and unauthorized access.

Image: AI impression of the birth of computing.

In the early days of computing, security measures primarily focused on physical security, such as locking computer rooms and restricting access to authorized personnel. However, as computer networks began to emerge, new challenges arose, prompting the development of cryptographic techniques to protect data transmission and communication. With the proliferation of interconnected computer systems and the growth of the internet in the 1980s and 1990s, cyberattacks became increasingly prevalent. Malicious actors began exploiting vulnerabilities in software and networks to gain unauthorized access, steal sensitive information, and disrupt critical services.

In response to the growing threat of computer viruses and malware, the first antivirus software programs were developed in the 1980s. These early antivirus tools aimed to detect and remove malicious code from infected systems, providing a rudimentary form of defence against cyber threats.

As cyber threats continued to evolve and escalate, the need for more robust cybersecurity measures became apparent. Governments, businesses, and organizations began developing formalized cybersecurity frameworks, standards, and best practices to protect their digital assets and infrastructure.

Securing Tomorrow's World: Exploring the Convergence of Cybersecurity, Quantum Computing and AI

Image: AI impression of the birth of antivirus software

In the 21st century, governments around the world started enacting legislation and regulations to address cybersecurity concerns and promote cyber resilience. Laws such as the European Union's General Data Protection Regulation (GDPR) and the United States' Cybersecurity Enhancement Act aimed to enhance data protection, strengthen cybersecurity practices, and improve incident response capabilities.

The growing demand for cybersecurity

solutions gave rise to a thriving cybersecurity industry comprised of technology vendors, service providers, consultants, and cybersecurity professionals. Today, the cybersecurity market encompasses a wide range of products and services, including firewalls, intrusion detection systems, encryption technologies, security analytics, and incident response tools. The field of cybersecurity is dynamic and constantly evolving in response to new threats, technologies, and vulnerabilities.

Image: AI artistic impression of cybersecurity evolution and innovation

Securing Tomorrow's World: Exploring the Convergence of Cybersecurity, Quantum Computing and AI

Cybersecurity professionals continually adapt and innovate to stay ahead of emerging threats, employing advanced techniques such as threat intelligence, machine learning, and behavioural analytics to detect and mitigate cyber risks.

The origins of cybersecurity can be traced back to the early days of computing, with its evolution driven by advancements in technology, the proliferation of cyber threats, and the collective efforts of governments, businesses, and cybersecurity professionals to protect digital assets and mitigate cyber risks in an increasingly connected world.

2 TODAY'S COMPUTERS

In the modern era, computers have become an indispensable part of daily life, permeating nearly every aspect of society, from business and education to entertainment and healthcare. Today's computers are the culmination of decades of technological innovation, driven by advances in hardware, software, and connectivity. Let's delve into the technology and capabilities that define today's computing landscape.

2.1 Processing Power and Memory

At the heart of every computer is its central processing unit (CPU), which serves as the brain of the system. Today's CPUs are incredibly powerful, featuring multiple cores and sophisticated architectures that enable them to execute billions of instructions per second.

Image: AI impression of a computer of today

High-performance CPUs from manufacturers like Intel, AMD, and ARM power a wide range of devices, from desktop computers and laptops to smartphones and servers.

Memory and storage are essential components of any computer system, enabling the storage and retrieval of data and programs. Random access memory (RAM) provides temporary storage for active programs and data, allowing for fast access and manipulation. Solid-state drives (SSDs) and hard disk drives (HDDs) serve as long-term storage solutions, offering large capacities and fast read/write speeds.

Graphics processing units (GPUs) have become increasingly important in modern computing, especially for tasks such as gaming, multimedia editing, and scientific computing. GPUs are highly parallel processors optimized for handling large datasets and performing complex calculations in parallel, making them well-suited for tasks that require high computational throughput.

2.2 Connectivity and Networking

The internet has revolutionized the way we communicate, collaborate, and access information, and modern computers are equipped with robust networking capabilities to facilitate seamless connectivity. Ethernet, Wi-Fi, Bluetooth, and cellular technologies enable computers to connect to local networks and the internet, empowering users to access a wealth of online resources and services.

Securing Tomorrow's World: Exploring the Convergence of Cybersecurity, Quantum Computing and AI

Image: AI impression of connectivity and networking

2.3 AI and Machine Learning

Artificial intelligence (AI) and machine learning (ML) have emerged as transformative technologies, driving innovation in areas such as natural language processing, image recognition, and autonomous systems. Today's computers are equipped with powerful AI accelerators and software frameworks that enable them to learn from data, recognize patterns, and make intelligent decisions in real-time. While still in its infancy, quantum computing holds the promise of revolutionizing computing as we know it. Quantum computers leverage the principles of quantum mechanics to perform computations that would be infeasible for classical computers, such as factoring large numbers and simulating quantum systems. Major technology companies and research institutions are investing heavily in quantum computing research, with the goal of unlocking its full potential in the years to come.

In an increasingly interconnected world, ensuring the security and privacy of computer systems and data is of paramount importance. Today's computers are equipped with advanced security features, including encryption, authentication, and intrusion detection systems, to protect against cyber threats such as malware, phishing, and data breaches. Additionally, privacy regulations and best practices help safeguard individuals' personal information and digital identities. User experience (UX) design plays a crucial role in shaping the interaction between humans and computers, with modern operating systems and software applications featuring intuitive interfaces and seamless workflows. Touchscreens, voice recognition, gesture controls, and augmented reality are just a few examples of the innovative interfaces that enhance the usability and accessibility of today's computers.

To summarise, today's computers are marvels of

engineering and innovation, embodying the collective efforts of scientists, engineers, and technologists to push the boundaries of what is possible. With ever-increasing processing power, storage capacity, and connectivity, computers have become indispensable tools for solving complex problems, driving economic growth, and enriching lives around the world.

2.4 The limits of the CPU

In the quest for ever-increasing performance and efficiency, the field of computer central processing unit (CPU) technology has made remarkable strides over the decades. However, despite these advancements, there are inherent limitations that pose challenges to further progress. Let's explore some of the key constraints on current CPU technology.

Image: AI impression of a powerful multicore CPU

Moore's Law, which states that the number of transistors on a microchip doubles approximately every two years, has been the driving force behind the exponential growth of computational power for several decades. However, as transistor sizes approach atomic scales and manufacturing processes reach physical limits, the ability to continue scaling transistors according to Moore's Law is becoming increasingly challenging. This phenomenon, known as Dennard scaling, has led to diminishing returns in terms of performance improvements and energy efficiency. As transistor densities have increased and clock speeds have risen, power consumption and heat dissipation have emerged as significant challenges in CPU design. The power consumption of modern CPUs can reach tens or even hundreds of watts, leading to issues such as thermal throttling, where CPUs reduce their clock speeds to prevent overheating. Additionally, the need for elaborate cooling solutions, such as heat sinks and fans, adds complexity and cost to CPU systems.

While CPUs have seen significant performance gains over the years, memory and data movement have not kept pace, leading to bottlenecks in CPU performance. Memory access latencies, cache misses, and memory bandwidth limitations can hinder the ability of CPUs to efficiently process data, especially in applications that require large datasets or intensive memory access patterns. This disparity between CPU processing power and memory performance is known as the "memory wall" and presents a fundamental challenge in computer architecture. Modern CPUs employ techniques such as instruction pipelining, out-of-order execution, and speculative execution to maximize instruction-level parallelism and improve performance. However, these techniques are subject to diminishing returns as the complexity and overhead associated with executing instructions in parallel increase. Furthermore, certain types of applications, such as single-threaded or serial workloads, may not benefit significantly from instruction-level parallelism, limiting the effectiveness of these techniques in certain scenarios.

As transistor sizes continue to shrink, quantum effects such as tunnelling and leakage currents become increasingly significant. Quantum tunnelling occurs when electrons "tunnel" through barriers in transistor gates, leading to unpredictable behaviour and increased power consumption. Leakage currents result from the flow of electrons through transistor channels even when they are supposed to be off, contributing to wasted energy and reduced reliability. These quantum effects pose fundamental challenges to transistor scaling and limit the minimum size and efficiency of transistors. The design and manufacturing of advanced CPUs require substantial investments in research, development, and fabrication facilities. As transistor scaling becomes more challenging and expensive, the cost-effectiveness of further advancements in CPU technology becomes increasingly uncertain. Economic factors, such as market demand, competition, and return on investment, can influence the pace and direction of CPU innovation, potentially limiting the scope of future advancements.

While current computer CPU technology has achieved remarkable levels of performance and efficiency, there are inherent limits that pose challenges to further progress. From the physical constraints of transistor scaling to the economic realities of manufacturing and market dynamics, navigating these limitations requires innovative solutions and strategic decision-making. As researchers and engineers continue to push the boundaries of CPU technology, addressing these challenges will be essential to unlocking new frontiers of computational power and efficiency.

3 3 SECURING THE PRESENT: CYBERSECURITY WITH TODAY'S COMPUTERS

In the digital age, cybersecurity is paramount to safeguarding sensitive information, protecting critical infrastructure, and preserving individual privacy. With cyber threats constantly evolving in sophistication and scale, adopting a comprehensive and proactive approach to cybersecurity is essential for organizations and individuals alike. Here are key strategies for securing digital assets with today's computers.

Conduct a thorough risk assessment to identify potential vulnerabilities and threats to your systems and data. This involves assessing the value of assets, evaluating existing security measures, and understanding potential attack vectors. By understanding the specific risks faced by your organization, you can prioritize resources and implement targeted security controls to mitigate these risks effectively.

Enforce robust authentication mechanisms to prevent unauthorized access to sensitive systems and data. This includes implementing multi-factor authentication (MFA) for user accounts, using strong and unique passwords, and regularly updating authentication credentials. By strengthening authentication practices, organizations can significantly reduce the risk of unauthorized access and credential-based attacks.

Encrypting sensitive data both at rest and in transit is essential for preserving confidentiality and integrity. Utilize encryption algorithms and protocols to secure data stored on servers, databases, and endpoints, as well as data transmitted over networks. Additionally, implement data loss prevention (DLP) solutions to monitor and control the movement of sensitive information within and outside the organization, further enhancing data protection measures.

Keep systems and software up-to-date with the latest security patches and updates to address known vulnerabilities and weaknesses. Establish a formal patch management process to regularly assess, prioritize, and deploy patches across the organization's IT infrastructure. Additionally, conduct vulnerability scanning and penetration testing to proactively identify and remediate security flaws before they can be exploited by malicious actors.

Segmenting network environments and implementing access controls are critical for limiting the impact of security incidents and containing unauthorized access. Employ firewalls, intrusion detection/prevention systems (IDS/IPS), and network segmentation techniques to create defence-in-depth architectures that segregate sensitive assets and restrict lateral movement by attackers within the network.

Invest in cybersecurity awareness training programs to educate employees about common threats, best practices, and security policies. Promote a culture of security consciousness by encouraging employees to report suspicious activities, adhere to security protocols, and exercise caution when interacting with emails, websites, and external devices. By empowering users with the knowledge and tools to recognize and respond to potential threats, organizations can strengthen their overall security posture.

Develop and maintain an incident response plan to effectively respond to security incidents and data breaches. Establish clear procedures for detecting, analysing, and containing security breaches, as well as for communicating with stakeholders and regulatory authorities. Conduct regular tabletop exercises and simulations to test the effectiveness of incident response procedures and ensure readiness to handle cybersecurity incidents.

Securing digital assets with today's computers requires a proactive and multi-layered approach that encompasses risk assessment, strong authentication, encryption, patch management, network segmentation, user education, and incident response planning. By implementing these key strategies and continuously adapting to emerging threats, organizations can mitigate cyber risks and protect against unauthorized access, data breaches, and other cybersecurity incidents.

4 QUANTUM COMPUTING: NEW BEGINNINGS

In the realm of computing, quantum technology stands at the threshold of a new era, promising to revolutionize the way we process information, solve complex problems, and understand the fundamental laws of the universe. Quantum computing harnesses the principles of quantum mechanics to perform computations that would be infeasible for classical computers, offering unparalleled computational power and potential. As we embark on this journey into the quantum realm, we find ourselves at the dawn of a new era of discovery and innovation.

4.1 Quantum Principles and Phenomena

At the heart of quantum computing lies the fascinating and often counterintuitive principles of quantum mechanics.

Securing Tomorrow's World: Exploring the Convergence of Cybersecurity, Quantum Computing and AI

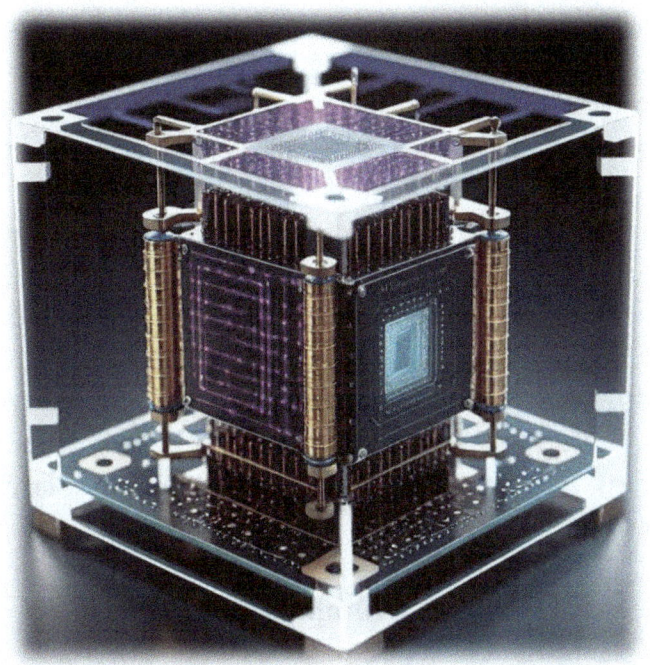

Image: AI impression of a quantum computer

Concepts such as superposition, entanglement, and interference form the foundation of quantum computing, enabling computations to be performed on qubits—quantum bits—that can exist in multiple states simultaneously. Unlike classical bits, which can only be in a state of 0 or 1, qubits can exist in a state of 0, 1, or any superposition of both states, exponentially increasing the computational capacity of quantum computers.

4.2 Quantum Hardware and Architectures

Quantum computers consist of physical systems capable of encoding, manipulating, and measuring quantum information. Various approaches to quantum hardware exist, including superconducting qubits, trapped ions, photonic qubits, and topological qubits, each with its own strengths and challenges. Quantum computers are typically housed in specialized facilities known as dilution refrigerators, which maintain ultra-low temperatures to protect delicate quantum states from decoherence—a process that disrupts quantum information and limits computation.

4.3 Quantum Algorithms and Applications

Quantum computing holds the potential to revolutionize fields ranging from cryptography and cybersecurity to drug discovery and materials science. Quantum algorithms, such as Shor's algorithm for integer factorization and Grover's algorithm for unstructured search, offer exponential speedups over classical algorithms for certain problem classes. Applications of quantum computing include simulating quantum systems, optimizing complex processes, and solving combinatorial optimization problems that are intractable for classical computers. In recent years, significant milestones have been achieved in the field of quantum computing, culminating in the demonstration of quantum supremacy—the ability of a quantum computer to outperform the most powerful classical supercomputers for certain tasks. Google's Sycamore processor, for example, achieved quantum supremacy by performing a calculation in minutes that would take classical supercomputers thousands of years to complete. These milestones mark a pivotal moment in the development of quantum technology and signal the dawn of a new era in computing.

Despite the tremendous progress made in quantum computing, significant challenges remain on the path to realizing practical, scalable quantum computers. Decoherence, noise, and error rates pose formidable obstacles to building reliable quantum hardware, while developing efficient quantum algorithms and error-correction techniques remains an active area of research. Additionally, bridging the gap between quantum hardware and real-world applications requires interdisciplinary collaboration and innovative solutions. As quantum computing continues to advance, it raises important societal implications and ethical considerations. Quantum cryptography, for example, offers the potential for unbreakable encryption and secure communication channels, but it also poses challenges for law enforcement and national security agencies. Additionally, the development of quantum computing technologies must be guided by principles of inclusivity, fairness, and accountability to ensure that the benefits of quantum technology are equitably distributed and responsibly managed.

Image: AI impression of quantum algorithms

Quantum computing represents a new frontier in the quest for computational power and scientific discovery. With its ability to tackle previously intractable problems and unlock new realms of knowledge, quantum technology holds the promise of transforming industries, driving innovation, and shaping the future of computing. As we embark on this journey into the quantum realm, we stand at the threshold of new beginnings, poised to explore the uncharted territories of the quantum universe, and unlock the mysteries of the cosmos.

5 QUANTUM CRYPTOGRAPHY OVERVIEW

Quantum cryptography is a branch of cryptography that leverages the principles of quantum mechanics to secure communication channels and exchange cryptographic keys with unprecedented levels of security. Unlike classical cryptographic techniques, which rely on mathematical algorithms and computational complexity, quantum cryptography offers provably secure methods for protecting sensitive information against eavesdropping and unauthorized access. Let's explore the key concepts, techniques, and applications of quantum cryptography.

At the heart of quantum cryptography lies the concept of quantum key distribution (QKD), which enables two parties to establish a shared cryptographic key over an insecure communication channel with the guarantee of unconditional security. QKD protocols, such as the BB84 protocol developed by Charles Bennett and Gilles Brassard, exploit the principles of quantum mechanics, including the Heisenberg uncertainty principle and the no-cloning theorem, to detect and thwart eavesdropping attempts.

Several QKD protocols have been developed to facilitate the secure exchange of cryptographic keys between parties. The BB84 protocol, E91 protocol, and the more recent measurement-device-independent QKD (MDI-QKD) protocol are among the most widely studied and implemented QKD schemes. These protocols rely on the transmission of quantum states, such as polarized photons or entangled particles, between the sender and receiver, followed by measurements to determine the shared key.

While the theoretical principles of quantum cryptography are well-established, practical implementations face several challenges, including technical limitations, environmental factors, and scalability issues. Real-world QKD systems must contend with issues such as photon loss, channel noise, and detector inefficiencies, which can degrade the performance and reliability of the cryptographic key exchange process. Additionally, integrating QKD into existing communication infrastructure presents logistical and compatibility challenges that require careful consideration.

Despite these challenges, quantum cryptography holds great promise for enhancing the security of communication networks, protecting sensitive data, and enabling new applications in fields such as finance, healthcare, and government. QKD technology is already being deployed in select applications, such as secure satellite communication links and high-security government networks. Looking ahead, ongoing research efforts aim to overcome existing limitations and expand the practical capabilities of quantum cryptography, paving the way for its widespread adoption and integration into mainstream communication systems.

5.1 Quantum Entanglement and Superposition

Quantum cryptography relies on the properties of quantum entanglement and superposition to ensure the security of cryptographic keys. Entangled qubits, which are particles whose quantum states are correlated with each other, enable the detection of eavesdropping by measuring the correlations between the transmitted and received qubits. Superposition allows qubits to exist in multiple states simultaneously, providing a means of encoding information in a way that is resistant to interception or interception.

Image: AI impression of quantum entanglement

5.2 Quantum Cryptography vs. Classical Cryptography

Quantum cryptography offers several advantages over classical cryptographic techniques, including unconditional security guarantees, resistance to quantum attacks, and the ability to detect eavesdropping with high probability. Unlike classical cryptographic algorithms, which may be vulnerable to attacks based on mathematical algorithms or computational complexity, quantum cryptography relies on the fundamental laws of physics to ensure the security of communication channels and cryptographic keys.

Quantum cryptography represents a groundbreaking approach to securing communication channels and protecting sensitive information against eavesdropping and interception. By harnessing the principles of quantum mechanics, QKD protocols offer provably secure methods for establishing cryptographic keys with unprecedented levels of security. As research and development efforts continue to advance, quantum cryptography is poised to play an increasingly vital role in safeguarding the integrity and confidentiality of communication networks in the digital age.

6 THE FUTURE: QUANTUM COMPUTING CYBERSECURITY

As the world rapidly progresses towards the era of quantum computing, the landscape of cybersecurity faces unprecedented challenges. Traditional cryptographic methods, which rely on the complexity of mathematical problems for security, are at risk of being rendered obsolete by the exponential computational power of quantum computers. To safeguard sensitive information and ensure data integrity in this new paradigm, a proactive and multifaceted approach to quantum computing cybersecurity is essential.

The concept of quantum computing can be traced back to the early 20th century with the development of quantum mechanics. Scientists such as Max Planck, Albert Einstein, Niels Bohr, and Erwin Schrödinger laid the theoretical groundwork by exploring the behaviour of particles at the quantum level. This foundational work led to the formulation of quantum mechanics, which describes the strange and counterintuitive properties of quantum systems, including superposition, entanglement, and uncertainty.

The idea of harnessing these quantum properties to perform computation was first proposed by physicist Richard Feynman in 1981. Feynman envisioned that quantum computers could simulate quantum systems with unprecedented efficiency, offering a powerful tool for scientific research and exploration. In 1985, physicist David Deutsch further developed the concept of quantum computation, introducing the notion of a universal quantum computer capable of solving a wide range of problems exponentially faster than classical computers.

The field of quantum computing saw significant progress in the 1990s with the development of experimental techniques for manipulating and controlling quantum systems. In 1994, mathematician Peter Shor devised a quantum algorithm for factoring large integers—a problem that is exponentially difficult for classical computers to solve. Shor's algorithm demonstrated the potential of quantum computers to break cryptographic systems based on integer factorization, sparking widespread interest and investment in quantum computing research.

In the early 21st century, researchers began making strides in building practical quantum computing hardware. Several approaches to implementing quantum bits, or qubits—the fundamental units of quantum information—were explored, including superconducting circuits, trapped ions, and semiconductor-based qubits. Companies and research institutions worldwide embarked on ambitious projects to develop scalable quantum processors capable of performing meaningful computations.

In 2019, Google claimed to have achieved a milestone known as "quantum supremacy" with its 53-qubit quantum processor, Sycamore. Google's experiment demonstrated that its quantum processor could perform a specific task—sampling from a random quantum circuit—faster than the most powerful classical supercomputers. While the achievement was hailed as a significant milestone in quantum computing, challenges remain in scaling up quantum systems, improving qubit coherence and error correction, and achieving practical quantum advantage for real-world applications.

Looking ahead, the potential applications of quantum computing span a wide range of fields, including cryptography, optimization, drug discovery, material science, and artificial intelligence. Quantum computers have the potential to revolutionize industries by solving complex problems that are currently intractable for classical computers. From accelerating drug discovery and optimizing supply chains to revolutionizing financial modelling and enhancing cybersecurity, quantum computing promises to unlock new frontiers in science, technology, and innovation.

Despite the progress made in quantum computing, significant challenges remain on the path to practical quantum advantage. Key challenges include decoherence, noise, error correction, qubit scalability, and the development of fault-tolerant quantum algorithms. Overcoming these challenges will require interdisciplinary collaboration between physicists, engineers, computer scientists, and mathematicians, as well as sustained investment in research and development.

As we look to the future, quantum computing holds the potential to usher in a new era of computing, transforming industries, driving innovation, and addressing some of the most pressing challenges facing society. However, realizing this vision will require continued investment, collaboration, and perseverance to overcome technical hurdles and unlock the full potential of quantum computing.

The history and future of quantum computing are characterized by remarkable progress, groundbreaking discoveries, and immense potential. From its theoretical foundations in quantum mechanics to experimental breakthroughs in quantum hardware, quantum computing has evolved into a vibrant and rapidly advancing field with profound implications for science, technology, and society.

7 UNDERSTANDING QUANTUM THREATS

First and foremost, organizations must comprehend the unique threats posed by quantum computing. Quantum computers have the potential to effortlessly crack widely used encryption algorithms such as RSA and ECC by exploiting their ability to perform complex calculations exponentially faster than classical computers. Recognizing this vulnerability is the first step towards developing effective countermeasures.

7.1 Post-Quantum Cryptography (PQC)

Transitioning to post-quantum cryptographic algorithms is paramount for maintaining data security in the quantum era. PQC algorithms are specifically designed to withstand attacks from both classical and quantum computers, making them essential for protecting sensitive information in the long term. Collaborative efforts between researchers, industry experts, and government agencies are crucial for the standardization and implementation of PQC algorithms across various platforms and systems.

Quantum key distribution offers a promising solution for achieving unconditional security in data transmission. Unlike traditional cryptographic methods, which rely on the complexity of mathematical problems, QKD leverages the principles of quantum mechanics to enable the secure exchange of encryption keys between parties. Implementing QKD protocols can significantly enhance the confidentiality and integrity of communication channels, thereby mitigating the risk of eavesdropping and interception by quantum adversaries.

The field of quantum computing and cybersecurity is constantly evolving, necessitating ongoing research and development efforts to stay ahead of emerging threats. Investing in research initiatives focused on quantum-resistant cryptography, quantum-safe protocols, and quantum-resistant hardware is essential for advancing the state-of-the-art in quantum computing cybersecurity. Collaborative partnerships between academia, industry, and government institutions are vital for driving innovation and fostering the development of robust security solutions.

Educating stakeholders about the implications of quantum computing on cybersecurity is critical for fostering a proactive security mindset. Organizations should prioritize training programs and awareness campaigns to ensure that employees, decision-makers, and the general public are equipped with the knowledge and resources to address quantum threats effectively. By fostering a culture of cybersecurity awareness and resilience, organizations can better protect themselves against evolving cyber threats in the quantum era.

Securing the future of cybersecurity in the age of quantum computing requires a comprehensive and proactive approach. By understanding quantum threats, transitioning to post-quantum cryptographic algorithms, implementing quantum key distribution protocols, fostering continuous research and development, and prioritizing education and awareness, organizations can mitigate the risks posed by quantum adversaries and safeguard sensitive information in the quantum era.

Securing Tomorrow's World: Exploring the Convergence of Cybersecurity, Quantum Computing and AI

Image: AI impression of cryptography

8 UNLEASHING THE POTENTIAL: THE FUTURE OF AI WITH QUANTUM COMPUTERS

Artificial intelligence (AI) has already revolutionized countless industries, from healthcare to finance, with its ability to analyse vast amounts of data, recognize patterns, and make predictions. As we look to the future, the convergence of AI and quantum computing holds the promise of unlocking even greater potential, enabling new capabilities and accelerating progress in AI research and applications.

Quantum computing offers the potential to revolutionize machine learning—the core technology driving many AI applications. Quantum machine learning algorithms leverage the unique properties of quantum systems, such as superposition and entanglement, to perform computations that are exponentially faster than classical counterparts. These algorithms can enhance tasks such as pattern recognition, natural language processing, and recommendation systems, enabling more accurate predictions and insights from complex datasets.

Neural networks are the backbone of modern AI, powering applications such as image recognition, speech synthesis, and autonomous vehicles. Quantum neural networks, built on quantum computing frameworks, promise to enhance the capabilities of traditional neural networks by leveraging quantum entanglement and interference to process information in new ways. Quantum neural networks could enable faster training, more efficient inference, and the ability to tackle previously unsolvable problems in AI research.

Optimization lies at the heart of many AI algorithms, from training neural networks to solving complex decision-making problems. Quantum optimization algorithms, such as quantum annealing and variational quantum algorithms, offer the potential to accelerate optimization tasks by leveraging quantum parallelism and tunnelling effects to explore vast solution spaces more efficiently. These algorithms have applications in fields such as logistics, finance, and drug discovery, where finding optimal solutions is critical.

Generative models are a class of AI algorithms used to generate new data samples that mimic the distribution of a given dataset. Quantum generative models, powered by quantum computing, could offer new capabilities for data generation and synthesis by leveraging quantum coherence to explore high-dimensional data spaces more effectively. These models could have applications in generating realistic images, designing novel molecules, and simulating quantum systems with unprecedented accuracy.

Reinforcement learning is a branch of machine learning focused on training agents to make sequential decisions to maximize cumulative rewards. Quantum reinforcement learning algorithms aim to enhance traditional reinforcement learning techniques by harnessing quantum computing resources to explore and exploit action spaces more efficiently. These algorithms could have applications in robotics, autonomous systems, and game playing, where agents must navigate complex environments and make decisions in real-time.

8.1 Quantum AI Hardware

In addition to algorithms and software, the future of AI with quantum computing also involves the development of specialized hardware optimized for AI tasks. Quantum AI processors, quantum annealers, and quantum-inspired accelerators could offer significant performance gains for AI workloads by leveraging the unique properties of quantum systems. These quantum AI hardware platforms could enable faster training, more efficient inference, and the development of AI models with higher accuracy and complexity.

As we explore the potential of AI with quantum computing, it is essential to consider the ethical, societal, and regulatory implications of these advancements. Issues such as algorithmic bias, data privacy, and the responsible use of AI must be addressed to ensure that AI technologies benefit society while minimizing potential harms. Ethical frameworks, transparency measures, and regulatory oversight are essential for guiding the responsible development and deployment of AI with quantum computing.

The future of AI with quantum computing holds tremendous promise for revolutionizing the field of artificial intelligence. From quantum machine learning and neural networks to optimization, generative models, and reinforcement learning, quantum computing has the potential to unlock new capabilities and accelerate progress in AI research and applications. By leveraging the unique properties of quantum systems, we can pave the way for a future where AI transforms industries, drives innovation, and enhances the human experience.

Image: AI artistic impression of Quantum AI

9 EXPLORING THE FUTURE FRONTIERS OF COMPUTING

Computing has undergone remarkable evolution since the advent of classical computers, and as we journey further into the 21st century, the landscape of computing continues to expand into uncharted territories. While quantum computing represents a significant milestone in computational power, researchers and innovators are already envisioning the next frontiers of computing beyond quantum systems.

While quantum computing holds promise for solving certain classes of problems exponentially faster than classical computers, it also poses significant challenges, including qubit coherence, error correction, and scalability. Post-quantum computing aims to address these challenges by exploring alternative paradigms and computational models that may offer practical advantages over quantum systems. This includes research into novel approaches such as adiabatic computing, topological quantum computing, and DNA computing, which leverage different physical substrates and computational principles to perform computation.

9.1 Neuromorphic Computing

Inspired by the structure and function of the human brain, neuromorphic computing seeks to develop computing systems that mimic the behaviour of neural networks. Unlike traditional von Neumann architectures, which separate memory and processing units, neuromorphic systems integrate memory and processing, enabling parallelism and efficiency akin to the brain's neural networks. Neuromorphic computing holds promise for tasks such as pattern recognition, machine learning, and cognitive computing, with potential applications in robotics, autonomous systems, and artificial intelligence.

Securing Tomorrow's World: Exploring the Convergence of Cybersecurity, Quantum Computing and AI

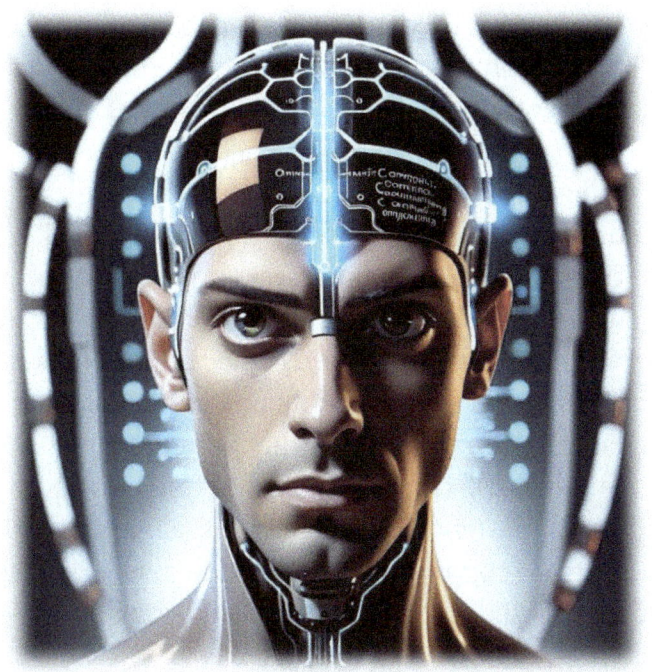

Image: AI artistic impression of neuromorphic computing

9.2 Theory for Cybersecurity of Neuromorphic Computing

Neuromorphic computing, inspired by the structure and function of the human brain, holds great promise for revolutionizing computing by enabling ultra-efficient, brain-like processing of information. As this transformative technology advances, ensuring robust cybersecurity measures is paramount to protect against potential vulnerabilities and threats. A comprehensive theory for cybersecurity of neuromorphic computing must address several key aspects.

To develop effective cybersecurity strategies for neuromorphic computing, it is essential to understand the architecture and operation of neuromorphic systems. Neuromorphic hardware typically consists of interconnected neurons or artificial synapses, organized in a massively parallel fashion to mimic the parallel processing capabilities of the brain. These systems rely on synaptic plasticity and spiking neural networks to perform cognitive tasks such as pattern recognition, learning, and decision-making.

A theory for cybersecurity of neuromorphic computing must identify potential threats and vulnerabilities specific to neuromorphic systems. These threats may include adversarial attacks targeting synaptic weights, hardware-level vulnerabilities exploiting physical defects or side-channel attacks, and software-level exploits exploiting weaknesses in neuromorphic algorithms or programming interfaces. By understanding the unique characteristics of neuromorphic systems, researchers can anticipate and mitigate potential threats more effectively. Secure neuromorphic algorithms are essential for ensuring the integrity, confidentiality, and availability of neuromorphic systems. Researchers must develop algorithms that are resilient to adversarial attacks, robust against noise and hardware faults, and capable of detecting and mitigating anomalies in real-time. Additionally, encryption techniques tailored for neuromorphic computing may be necessary to protect sensitive data and prevent unauthorized access.

Securing the hardware components of neuromorphic systems is crucial for protecting against physical attacks and tampering. Hardware-level security measures may include techniques such as tamper-resistant packaging, secure bootstrapping, and Physical Unclonable Functions (PUFs) to ensure the authenticity and integrity of neuromorphic chips. Additionally, hardware-based encryption and authentication mechanisms can safeguard communication channels and prevent unauthorized access to sensitive information. Building trustworthy neuromorphic ecosystems requires collaboration between hardware manufacturers, software developers, researchers, and regulatory bodies. Standards and certification processes for neuromorphic hardware and software can help establish trust and confidence in the security and reliability of neuromorphic systems. Additionally, transparent and accountable governance frameworks are essential for addressing ethical, legal, and societal concerns related to neuromorphic computing.

Cybersecurity for neuromorphic computing is an ongoing process that requires continuous monitoring, assessment, and adaptation to evolving threats and vulnerabilities. Researchers and practitioners must remain vigilant and proactive in detecting and responding to emerging cyber threats, leveraging techniques such as anomaly detection, intrusion prevention, and threat intelligence to safeguard neuromorphic systems effectively. Additionally, regular security audits and penetration testing can help identify weaknesses and validate the effectiveness of cybersecurity measures.

Collaboration and knowledge sharing are essential for advancing cybersecurity research and practice in the field of neuromorphic computing. Establishing interdisciplinary research collaborations between cybersecurity experts, neuromorphic researchers, and industry stakeholders can facilitate the development of innovative security solutions and best practices. Open-source initiatives and community-driven platforms can also promote knowledge sharing and dissemination of cybersecurity insights and tools within the neuromorphic computing community.

A comprehensive theory for cybersecurity of neuromorphic computing must address the unique challenges and opportunities posed by this transformative technology. By understanding the architecture of neuromorphic systems, identifying potential threats and vulnerabilities, developing secure algorithms, implementing hardware-level security measures, establishing trustworthy ecosystems, and fostering collaboration and knowledge sharing, we can build resilient and trustworthy neuromorphic computing systems that enable a safer and more secure future.

9.3 Quantum-Inspired Computing

While fully-fledged quantum computers remain a distant goal, quantum-inspired computing represents an intermediate step towards harnessing quantum principles for practical computation. Quantum-inspired algorithms and algorithms inspired by quantum mechanics are designed to run on classical hardware but exploit quantum-like effects such as superposition, entanglement, and interference to achieve computational speedups. These algorithms have shown promise for optimization problems, machine learning, and cryptography, offering a bridge between classical and quantum computing paradigms.

9.4 Molecular and DNA Computing

Molecular and DNA computing leverage the inherent properties of molecules and DNA molecules for computation. By encoding information in the structure and sequence of molecules, researchers aim to perform parallel computation on massive scales, surpassing the limitations of classical and even quantum systems. Molecular and DNA computing hold potential for solving complex optimization problems, simulating biological processes, and designing novel materials with tailored properties.

Securing Tomorrow's World: Exploring the Convergence of Cybersecurity, Quantum Computing and AI

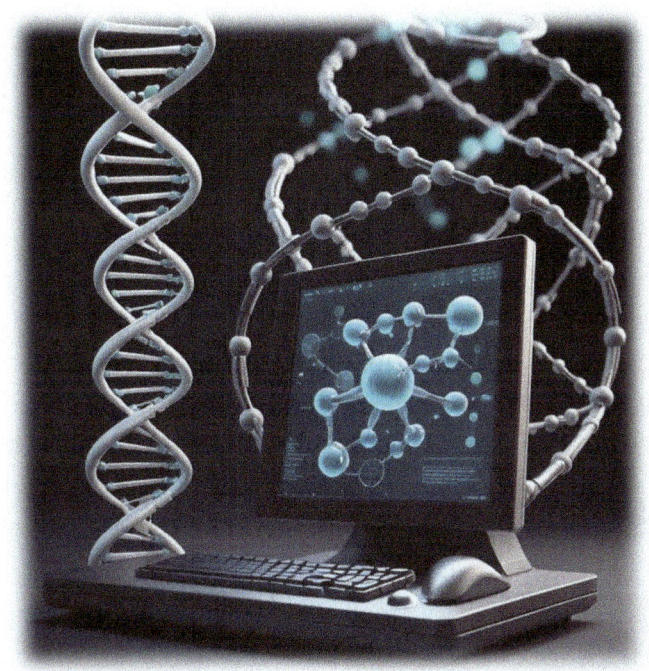

Image: AI artistic impression of molecular and DNA computing

9.5 Theory for Cybersecurity of Molecular and DNA Computing

Molecular and DNA computing harness the unique properties of molecules and DNA molecules to perform computation, offering the potential for ultra-fast, massively parallel processing of information. As this groundbreaking technology continues to advance, robust cybersecurity measures are essential to protect against potential threats and vulnerabilities. A comprehensive theory for cybersecurity of molecular and DNA computing must address several key aspects.

To develop effective cybersecurity strategies for molecular and DNA computing, it is essential to understand the underlying principles and paradigms of these technologies. Molecular computing utilizes chemical reactions and molecular interactions to perform computation, while DNA computing relies on the sequence-specific hybridization of DNA molecules to encode and process information. Both paradigms offer unique advantages, such as parallelism, scalability, and energy efficiency, but also pose challenges in terms of reliability, error correction, and security.

A theory for cybersecurity of molecular and DNA computing must identify potential threats and vulnerabilities specific to these technologies. Threats may include adversarial attacks targeting molecular reactions or DNA sequences, manipulation of chemical inputs or outputs, and exploitation of physical or chemical properties to disrupt computation or compromise data integrity. Additionally, vulnerabilities in molecular and DNA computing algorithms, protocols, and hardware implementations must be addressed to mitigate potential risks effectively.

Secure algorithms are essential for ensuring the integrity, confidentiality, and availability of molecular and DNA computing systems. Researchers must develop algorithms that are resilient to adversarial attacks, robust against errors and noise inherent in molecular and DNA processes, and capable of detecting and mitigating anomalies in real-time. Additionally, encryption techniques tailored for molecular and DNA computing may be necessary to protect sensitive data and prevent unauthorized access.

Securing the hardware components of molecular and DNA computing systems is crucial for protecting against physical attacks and tampering. Hardware-level security measures may include techniques such as tamper-resistant packaging, secure bootstrapping, and physical unclonable functions (PUFs) to ensure the authenticity and integrity of molecular and DNA computing devices. Additionally, hardware-based encryption and authentication mechanisms can safeguard communication channels and prevent unauthorized access to sensitive information.

Building trustworthy molecular and DNA

computing ecosystems requires collaboration between researchers, manufacturers, regulatory bodies, and end-users. Standards and certification processes for molecular and DNA computing hardware and software can help establish trust and confidence in the security and reliability of these systems. Additionally, transparent and accountable governance frameworks are essential for addressing ethical, legal, and societal concerns related to molecular and DNA computing.

Cybersecurity for molecular and DNA computing is an ongoing process that requires continuous monitoring, assessment, and adaptation to evolving threats and vulnerabilities. Researchers and practitioners must remain vigilant and proactive in detecting and responding to emerging cyber threats, leveraging techniques such as anomaly detection, intrusion prevention, and threat intelligence to safeguard molecular and DNA computing systems effectively. Additionally, regular security audits and penetration testing can help identify weaknesses and validate the effectiveness of cybersecurity measures.

Collaboration and knowledge sharing are essential for advancing cybersecurity research and practice in the field of molecular and DNA computing. Establishing interdisciplinary research collaborations between cybersecurity experts, molecular biologists, DNA computing researchers, and industry stakeholders can facilitate the development of innovative security solutions and best practices. Open-source initiatives and community-driven platforms can also promote knowledge sharing and dissemination of cybersecurity insights and tools within the molecular and DNA computing community.

A comprehensive theory for cybersecurity of molecular and DNA computing must address the unique challenges and opportunities posed by these transformative technologies. By understanding the principles of molecular and DNA computing, identifying potential threats and vulnerabilities, developing secure algorithms, implementing hardware-level security measures, establishing trustworthy ecosystems, and fostering collaboration and knowledge sharing, we can build resilient and trustworthy molecular and DNA computing systems that enable a more secure future.

9.6 Photonic Computing

Photonic computing harnesses the properties of

light to perform computation, offering advantages such as high speed, low energy consumption, and immunity to electromagnetic interference. Photonic devices, such as optical switches, modulators, and detectors, enable the manipulation and transmission of data using photons instead of electrons, paving the way for ultra-fast and energy-efficient computing systems.

Photonic computing holds promise for applications in telecommunications, data centres, and high-performance computing.

9.7 Theory for Cybersecurity of Photonic Computing

Photonic computing harnesses the properties of light to perform computation, offering advantages such as high speed, low energy consumption, and immunity to electromagnetic interference. As this transformative technology continues to advance, robust cybersecurity measures are essential to protect against potential threats and vulnerabilities. A comprehensive theory for cybersecurity of photonic computing must address several key aspects.

Securing Tomorrow's World: Exploring the Convergence of Cybersecurity, Quantum Computing and AI

Image: AI impression of photonic computing

To develop effective cybersecurity strategies for photonic computing, it is essential to understand the architecture and operation of photonic systems. Photonic computing systems typically consist of optical components such as lasers, modulators, detectors, and waveguides, which manipulate and transmit light signals to perform computation. These systems offer unique advantages, including parallelism, bandwidth, and speed, but also pose challenges in terms of security, reliability, and integration with traditional computing infrastructures.

A theory for cybersecurity of photonic computing must identify potential threats and vulnerabilities specific to photonic systems. Threats may include attacks targeting optical components or communication channels, manipulation of light signals to disrupt computation or compromise data integrity, and exploitation of physical or electromagnetic properties to eavesdrop on data transmission. Additionally, vulnerabilities in photonic computing algorithms, protocols, and hardware implementations must be addressed to mitigate potential risks effectively.

Secure algorithms are essential for ensuring the integrity, confidentiality, and availability of photonic computing systems. Researchers must develop algorithms that are resilient to adversarial attacks, robust against noise and interference in optical channels, and capable of detecting and mitigating anomalies in real-time. Additionally, encryption techniques tailored for photonic computing may be necessary to protect sensitive data and prevent unauthorized access.

Securing the hardware components of photonic computing systems is crucial for protecting against physical attacks and tampering.

Hardware-level security measures may include techniques such as tamper-resistant packaging, secure key generation and distribution, and physical layer encryption to ensure the authenticity and integrity of photonic devices. Additionally, hardware-based authentication mechanisms can safeguard communication channels and prevent unauthorized access to sensitive information.

Building trustworthy photonic computing ecosystems requires collaboration between researchers, manufacturers, regulatory bodies, and end-users. Standards and certification processes for photonic computing hardware and software can help establish trust and confidence in the security and reliability of these systems. Additionally, transparent and accountable governance frameworks are essential for addressing ethical, legal, and societal concerns related to photonic computing.

Cybersecurity for photonic computing is an ongoing process that requires continuous monitoring, assessment, and adaptation to evolving threats and vulnerabilities. Researchers and practitioners must remain vigilant and proactive in detecting and responding to emerging cyber threats, leveraging techniques such as anomaly detection, intrusion prevention, and threat intelligence to safeguard photonic computing systems effectively. Additionally, regular security audits and penetration testing can help identify weaknesses and validate the effectiveness of cybersecurity measures.

Collaboration and knowledge sharing are, once again, essential for advancing cybersecurity research and practice in the field of photonic computing. Establishing interdisciplinary research collaborations between cybersecurity experts, photonics researchers, optical engineers, and industry stakeholders can facilitate the development of innovative security solutions and best practices. Open-source initiatives and community-driven platforms can also promote knowledge sharing and dissemination of cybersecurity insights and tools within the photonic computing community.

A more detailed theory for cybersecurity of photonic computing must consider the unique challenges and opportunities posed by this transformative technology. By understanding the underlying principles of photonic computing, identifying potential threats and vulnerabilities, developing secure algorithms, implementing hardware-level security measures, establishing trustworthy ecosystems, and fostering collaboration and knowledge sharing, we can build resilient and trustworthy photonic computing systems.

9.8 Hybrid and Heterogeneous Computing

Hybrid and heterogeneous computing architectures combine diverse computing technologies, such as classical processors, quantum processors, neuromorphic chips, and specialized accelerators, into unified systems. By leveraging the strengths of different computing paradigms, hybrid and heterogeneous systems can tackle a wide range of workloads and applications, from traditional computational tasks to emerging AI and scientific simulations. These architectures offer flexibility, scalability, and performance optimization, enabling the development of versatile and powerful computing platforms for the future.

Image: AI impression of hybrid and heterogeneous computers

As computing technologies continue to advance, it is essential to consider the ethical, societal, and environmental implications of these developments. Issues such as data privacy, algorithmic bias, cybersecurity, and sustainability must be addressed to ensure that computing technologies benefit humanity while minimizing potential harms. Ethical frameworks, regulations, and interdisciplinary collaboration are again essential for guiding the responsible development and deployment of future computing systems.

The future of computing beyond quantum computers is a rich tapestry of innovation, exploration, and discovery. From post-quantum and quantum-inspired computing to neuromorphic, molecular, and photonic computing, the next frontiers of computing offer exciting opportunities to push the boundaries of what is possible and revolutionize how we solve problems, process information, and interact with the world.

9.9 Theory for Cybersecurity of Hybrid and Heterogeneous Computing

Hybrid and heterogeneous computing architectures combine diverse computing technologies, such as classical processors, quantum processors, neuromorphic chips, and specialized accelerators, into unified systems. These architectures offer versatility, scalability, and performance optimization, enabling the development of powerful computing platforms for a wide range of applications. However, ensuring robust cybersecurity measures is essential to protect against potential threats and vulnerabilities. A comprehensive theory for cybersecurity of hybrid and heterogeneous computing must address several key aspects.

To develop effective cybersecurity strategies for hybrid and heterogeneous computing, it is essential to understand the architecture and operation of these systems. Hybrid computing architectures integrate multiple types of processing units, such as CPUs, GPUs, FPGAs, and AI accelerators, to perform different types of computation in parallel or sequentially. Heterogeneous computing architectures combine diverse computing technologies, such as classical and quantum processors, neuromorphic chips, and photonic devices, to leverage the strengths of each technology for specific tasks. These architectures offer unique advantages in terms of performance, flexibility, and energy efficiency but also pose challenges in terms of security, compatibility, and resource management.

A theory for cybersecurity of hybrid and heterogeneous computing must identify potential threats and vulnerabilities specific to these architectures. Threats may include attacks targeting communication interfaces between different processing units, exploitation of vulnerabilities in software layers or virtualization techniques used to manage heterogeneous resources, and manipulation of data or computations across multiple computing technologies. Additionally, vulnerabilities in hardware components, firmware, or middleware layers must be addressed to mitigate potential risks effectively. Secure software and middleware are essential for ensuring the integrity, confidentiality, and availability of hybrid and heterogeneous computing systems. Researchers must develop software and middleware solutions that are resilient to adversarial attacks, robust against vulnerabilities in underlying hardware or communication channels, and capable of detecting and mitigating anomalies in real-time. Additionally, encryption techniques, access controls, and authentication mechanisms may be necessary to protect sensitive data and prevent unauthorized access.

Securing the hardware components of hybrid and heterogeneous computing systems is crucial for protecting against physical attacks and tampering. Hardware-level security measures may include techniques such as hardware-based encryption, secure bootstrapping, and trusted execution environments to ensure the authenticity and integrity of computing resources. Additionally, hardware-based authentication mechanisms can safeguard communication channels and prevent unauthorized access to sensitive information.

Building trustworthy ecosystems and supply chains is essential for ensuring the security and reliability of hybrid and heterogeneous computing systems. Manufacturers, vendors, and suppliers must adhere to industry standards and best practices for hardware and software development, testing, and deployment. Additionally, transparent and accountable governance frameworks are essential for addressing ethical, legal, and societal concerns related to hybrid and heterogeneous computing.

Cybersecurity for hybrid and heterogeneous computing is an ongoing process that requires continuous monitoring, assessment, and adaptation to evolving threats and vulnerabilities. Researchers and practitioners must remain vigilant and proactive in detecting and responding to emerging cyber threats, leveraging techniques such as anomaly detection, intrusion prevention, and threat intelligence to safeguard computing systems effectively. Additionally, regular security audits and penetration testing can help identify weaknesses and validate the effectiveness of cybersecurity measures. Collaboration and knowledge sharing are essential for advancing cybersecurity research and practice in the field of hybrid and heterogeneous computing. Establishing interdisciplinary research collaborations between cybersecurity experts, computer scientists, hardware engineers, and industry stakeholders can facilitate the development of innovative security solutions and best practices. Open-source initiatives and community-driven platforms can also promote knowledge sharing and dissemination of cybersecurity insights and tools within the hybrid and heterogeneous computing community.

A more expanded theory for cybersecurity of hybrid and heterogeneous computing must address the unique challenges and opportunities posed by these transformative architectures. By understanding the principles of hybrid and heterogeneous computing, identifying potential threats and vulnerabilities, developing secure software and middleware, implementing hardware-level security measures, establishing trustworthy ecosystems, and fostering collaboration and knowledge sharing, we can build resilient and trustworthy computing systems for the future.

9.10 Exploring Extraterrestrial Computing: Bridging the Cosmic Divide

In our quest to unravel the mysteries of the universe, humanity has often looked to the stars for inspiration and insight. From the far reaches of outer space to the depths of alien worlds, the cosmos holds untold secrets waiting to be discovered. In recent years, the concept of extraterrestrial computing has emerged as a fascinating frontier in the intersection of space exploration, computing technology, and artificial intelligence.

Image: AI impression of an extra-terrestrial computer in a space based laboratory

Space-based computing refers to the utilization of computational resources in outer space, either on spacecraft, satellites, or extraterrestrial habitats. With advancements in miniaturization, power efficiency, and radiation-hardened electronics, space agencies and private companies are increasingly deploying computing systems in orbit to support various missions, from Earth observation and telecommunications to planetary exploration and scientific research.

While space-based computing offers unique advantages such as reduced latency, improved data processing capabilities, and enhanced autonomy for spacecraft, it also presents significant challenges. Harsh radiation environments, limited power and cooling resources, and communication constraints pose obstacles to the development and operation of spaceborne computing systems. Additionally, the vast distances and communication delays inherent in interplanetary exploration require innovative approaches to data storage, processing, and transmission.

Extraterrestrial computing has myriad applications in space exploration, enabling missions to gather, process, and analyse vast amounts of data in real-time. Spacecraft equipped with onboard computing capabilities can autonomously navigate through asteroid fields, analyse geological features on distant planets, and monitor the health of astronauts during long-duration space missions. Additionally, distributed computing networks involving interconnected satellites or lunar and Martian habitats could enable collaborative data processing and decision-making in space.

Artificial intelligence (AI) and robotics play crucial roles in enabling autonomous exploration and operation of space-based computing systems. AI algorithms can analyse sensor data, detect anomalies, and make decisions in dynamic and uncertain environments, reducing the need for human intervention. Robotic systems equipped with AI capabilities can perform tasks such as assembling structures in space, repairing spacecraft components, and exploring hazardous terrain on other planets, enhancing the efficiency and safety of space missions.

As humanity's reach extends beyond our solar system, the concept of interstellar communication and computing becomes increasingly relevant. Extraterrestrial civilizations may employ advanced computing technologies to transmit and receive signals across vast distances, enabling communication and collaboration on a cosmic scale. While the Search for Extra-Terrestrial Intelligence (SETI) remains ongoing, developments in quantum computing, optical communications, and deep space exploration could pave the way for interstellar computing networks in the future.

As we contemplate the possibilities of extraterrestrial computing, it is essential to consider the ethical, legal, and societal implications of our endeavours. Issues such as data privacy, security, and environmental sustainability must be addressed to ensure responsible exploration and utilization of space-based computing resources. Additionally, international cooperation, transparency, and inclusivity are essential for fostering collaboration and promoting the peaceful exploration and utilization of outer space.

As technology continues to advance and humanity's presence in space expands, the future of extraterrestrial computing holds boundless potential for discovery and innovation. From space-based AI and robotics to interstellar communication networks, the convergence of computing technology and space exploration promises to reshape our understanding of the cosmos and our place within it. By harnessing the power of extraterrestrial computing, we can unlock new frontiers of knowledge and embark on a journey of exploration and discovery that transcends the boundaries of our home planet.

Image: AI impression of space-based AI and robotics

Extraterrestrial computing represents a bold step towards unlocking the mysteries of the universe and realizing humanity's aspirations for space exploration and discovery. By embracing innovation, collaboration, and responsible stewardship, we can harness the power of computing technology to traverse the cosmic divide and chart a course towards a future among the stars.

10 EXPLORING THE POTENTIAL THREAT TO HUMANITY'S SURVIVAL

As humanity stands on the cusp of a new technological frontier marked by the convergence of quantum computing and artificial intelligence (AI), questions arise about the potential implications of this convergence for the future of our species. While both quantum computing and AI hold tremendous promise for advancing scientific discovery, solving complex problems, and improving our quality of life, there are legitimate concerns about the potential risks and challenges they pose to humanity's survival.

10.1 Unprecedented Computational Power

The convergence of quantum computing and AI could usher in an era of unprecedented computational power, enabling machines to process vast amounts of data and perform complex calculations at speeds far beyond the capabilities of current technologies. While this presents exciting opportunities for innovation and discovery, it also raises concerns about the potential for misuse or unintended consequences.

Image: AI impression of a futuristic government office building

10.2 Autonomous Decision-Making

AI systems empowered by quantum computing

could possess advanced capabilities for autonomous decision-making and problem-solving, raising ethical questions about their alignment with human values and interests. Without proper safeguards and oversight, autonomous AI systems could make decisions that have far-reaching implications for society, potentially leading to unintended harm or conflict.

10.3 Security Risks and Vulnerabilities

The convergence of quantum computing and AI introduces new security risks and vulnerabilities that could threaten the integrity of critical systems and infrastructure. Quantum computers have the potential to break existing cryptographic protocols and encryption schemes, exposing sensitive information to unauthorized access or manipulation. AI-powered cyberattacks could exploit vulnerabilities in quantum computing systems, leading to widespread disruption and chaos.

10.4 Existential Risks and Unforeseen Consequences

The combination of advanced AI algorithms and quantum computing capabilities raises concerns about the potential for existential risks and unforeseen consequences that could threaten humanity's survival. As AI systems become increasingly autonomous and intelligent, they may exhibit behaviours that are difficult to predict or control, leading to scenarios where human values and objectives are compromised or undermined.

The convergence of quantum computing and AI also poses profound ethical and societal implications that must be carefully considered. Questions of equity, fairness, and accountability arise as AI systems gain greater autonomy and decision-making authority. Additionally, concerns about job displacement, economic inequality, and the concentration of power in the hands of a few AI-driven entities warrant attention and proactive measures to mitigate potential negative outcomes.

Addressing the potential threats posed by the convergence of quantum computing and AI requires robust regulatory frameworks and governance mechanisms that balance innovation with safety and security. Governments, policymakers, and international organizations must work collaboratively to establish guidelines, standards, and norms for the responsible development and deployment of quantum computing and AI technologies.

10.5 Mitigating Risks and Ensuring Human-Centric AI

To mitigate the risks associated with the convergence of quantum computing and AI, it is imperative to prioritize human-centric approaches to technology development and deployment. This includes incorporating ethical considerations, transparency, and accountability into the design and implementation of AI systems, as well as fostering interdisciplinary collaboration and public engagement to ensure that the benefits of these technologies are equitably distributed and responsibly managed.

While the convergence of quantum computing and AI holds immense potential for advancing human knowledge and capabilities, it also poses significant challenges and risks to humanity's survival. By proactively addressing these concerns and adopting a human-centric approach to technology development, we can harness the transformative power of quantum computing and AI for the benefit of society while safeguarding against potential threats to our collective well-being and survival.

Securing Tomorrow's World: Exploring the Convergence of Cybersecurity, Quantum Computing and AI

Image: AI impression of futuristic human-centric AI

11 EPILOGUE: CHARTING THE PATH FORWARD

As we reach the conclusion of our journey through the convergence of cybersecurity, quantum computing, and artificial intelligence, we find ourselves at a pivotal moment in human history. The rapid pace of technological advancement has brought us to the threshold of a new era—one defined by unprecedented challenges and opportunities. In "Securing Tomorrow's World: Exploring the Convergence of Cybersecurity, Quantum Computing and AI " we have explored the intricate interplay between these transformative technologies, delving into their potential impact on society, governance, and the very fabric of human existence.

Throughout these pages, we have witnessed the profound implications of quantum computing, AI-driven cybersecurity, and their convergence for the future of humanity. From the promises

of quantum cryptography and secure communication to the ethical dilemmas posed by autonomous AI systems, our exploration has illuminated the complex dynamics shaping our digital landscape. We have grappled with questions of trust, privacy, and accountability in an age of ever-increasing connectivity and computational power, confronting the inherent tensions between innovation and
security, progress and peril.

As we reflect on the insights gleaned from our exploration, it becomes clear that securing tomorrow's world requires more than just technological solutions—it demands a holistic approach that integrates technical expertise with ethical considerations, regulatory frameworks, and human-centric values. We must strive to harness the transformative potential of quantum computing, AI, and cybersecurity while safeguarding against their unintended consequences and ensuring that the benefits of these technologies are equitably distributed. The challenges ahead are formidable, but so too are the opportunities for progress and advancement. By embracing innovation, fostering collaboration, and upholding our shared commitment to security and resilience, we can navigate the complexities of our digital age with wisdom, foresight, and resilience. Together, we can shape a future where technology serves as a

Image: AI impression of tomorrow's world

force for good, empowering individuals, organizations, and societies to thrive in an ever-changing world.

As we bid farewell to "Securing Tomorrow's World: Exploring the Convergence of Cybersecurity, Quantum Computing and AI" let us carry forward the lessons learned and the insights gained, embarking on a collective journey toward a brighter, more secure future for generations to come. The convergence of cybersecurity, quantum computing, and AI represents not just the culmination of decades of scientific inquiry, but the dawn of a new chapter in the story of humanity—a chapter filled with promise, possibility, and endless potential.

The future is ours to secure.

Leonardo da Vinci (1452-1519)

Renowned for his artistic genius, Leonardo da Vinci was also a prolific inventor and visionary thinker. His designs and sketches laid the groundwork for innovations in engineering, anatomy, and flight, including concepts for flying machines, armoured vehicles, and hydraulic systems.

Johannes Gutenberg (c. 1400-1468)

Inventor of the printing press, Johannes Gutenberg revolutionized the dissemination of information and the spread of knowledge by making books more affordable and accessible. The Gutenberg Bible, printed in the 1450s, is considered one of the most significant books in history.

Isaac Newton (1643-1727)

A towering figure in the history of science, Isaac Newton made groundbreaking contributions to physics, mathematics, and astronomy. His laws of motion, universal gravitation, and calculus laid the foundation for classical mechanics and profoundly influenced our understanding of the natural world.

Thomas Edison (1847-1931)

Often referred to as "The Wizard of Menlo Park," Thomas Edison was one of the most prolific inventors in history, holding over 1,000 patents. His inventions, including the phonograph, the electric light bulb, and the motion picture camera, transformed modern life and ushered in the age of electricity.

Nikola Tesla (1856-1943)

A visionary inventor and electrical engineer, Nikola Tesla made significant contributions to the development of alternating current (AC) electricity systems, wireless communication, and electric motors. His inventions and ideas laid the groundwork for numerous technologies that continue to shape the modern world.

Securing Tomorrow's World: Exploring the Convergence of Cybersecurity, Quantum Computing and AI

Alexander Graham Bell (1847-1922)

Credited with inventing the telephone, Alexander Graham Bell revolutionized communication by enabling voice transmission over long distances. His invention laid the foundation for the telecommunications industry and paved the way for future innovations in wireless communication.

Marie Curie (1867-1934)

A pioneering physicist and chemist, Marie Curie made groundbreaking discoveries in radioactivity and won Nobel Prizes in both physics and chemistry. Her research laid the groundwork for advancements in nuclear physics, medical imaging, and cancer treatment.

Alan Turing (1912-1954)

Considered the father of modern computer science, Alan Turing made foundational contributions to the development of theoretical computer science, artificial intelligence, and cryptography. His work on the Enigma code-breaking machine during World War II played a crucial role in Allied victory.

Tim Berners-Lee (1955-present)

Inventor of the World Wide Web, Tim Berners-Lee revolutionized communication and information sharing by creating a global system for accessing and sharing information over the internet. His invention laid the foundation for the modern internet and transformed the way we interact, learn, and conduct business.

Steve Jobs (1955-2011) and Steve Wozniak (1950-present)

Co-founders of Apple Inc., Steve Jobs and Steve Wozniak revolutionized the personal computer industry with the introduction of the Apple I and Apple II computers. Their innovations in user-friendly design, graphical interfaces, and software applications helped popularize personal computing and set the stage for the digital revolution.

Aeron P. White

www.ingramcontent.com/pod-product-compliance
Lightning Source LLC
Chambersburg PA
CBHW070307230526
45470CB00002B/764